PICKUP TRUCKS

Motor Mania

by Jeffrey Zuehlke

Mike Mueller, consultant, automotive writer and photographer

Lerner Publications Company • Minneapolis

Special thanks to Mike Mueller for his expertise and wonderful photos

For Uncle Freddy, the Truck Man

Cover Photo: A 2000 Dodge Dakota R/T with a custom paint job

Copyright © 2007 by Lerner Publications Company

Lerner Publications Company
A division of Lerner Publishing Group
241 First Avenue North
Minneapolis, MN 55401 U.S.A.

Website address: www.lernerbooks.com

Library of Congress Cataloging-in-Publication Data

Zuehlke, Jeffrey, 1968–
      Pickup trucks / by Jeffrey Zuehlke.
         p.   cm. — (Motor mania)
      Includes bibliographical references and index.
      ISBN-13: 978–0–8225–6564–2 (lib. bdg. : alk. paper)
      ISBN-10: 0–8225–6564–1 (lib. bdg. : alk. paper)
      1. Pickup trucks—Juvenile literature. I. Title.
    TL230.15.Z84 2007
    629.223'2—dc22   2006018811

Manufactured in the United States of America
1 2 3 4 5 6 – DP – 12 11 10 09 08 07

Contents

Introduction—What Is a Pickup Truck? 4

Chapter One—Pickup Truck History 6

Chapter Two—Pickup Truck Culture 22

Pickup Truck Gallery 34

Glossary 46

Selected Bibliography 46

Further Reading 46

Websites 46

Index 47

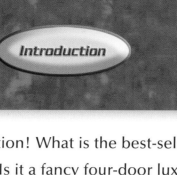

Quick question! What is the best-selling vehicle in the United States? Is it a fancy four-door luxury sedan? Is it a fast sports car? How about a roomy sport-utility vehicle (SUV)? Actually, none of these is correct. The best-selling vehicle in the United States is . . . a pickup truck, the Ford F-150.

What is a pickup truck exactly? It's an automobile with a cab for the driver and passengers and a large bed, or box, in back to hold cargo. It's a truck for picking up and carrying light-weight loads. (Light-duty truck is another term for this kind of vehicle.) For many people, however, pickup trucks are much more than vehicles. They are symbols of pride and style.

This is a far cry from how pickups used to be seen. In the early 1900s, trucks were workhorses and not much else. They were basic machines built to haul, tow, and do other kinds of dirty work. If the driver could fit behind the wheel without too much discomfort, that was enough. If the truck could reach 30 miles (48 kilometers) per hour, that was plenty fast.

Pickups have changed a lot since then. Modern trucks aren't just built to work hard. They look good doing it. Truck cabs have all the latest comforts. And some modern trucks are as fast as just about any car on the road.

Ford's F-series pickups, such as the F-150, have been the most popular trucks in the United States since the 1970s. Other top-selling pickup truck models are the Chevy Silverado and the Dodge Ram.

Chapter One

PICKUP TRUCK HISTORY

Horse-drawn wagons line a busy street in Boston, Massachusetts, around 1895.

It's a challenge as old as humankind—hauling you and your stuff from one place to another. For thousands of years, people used animals to do the job. Horses, mules, donkeys, camels—even elephants—have been the beasts of burden.

In the early history of the United States, horses or oxen were usually the working animals of choice. They helped pull the plows that tilled farmland. They hauled the wagons that carried the pioneers who settled in the West. Horses and horse-drawn wagons carried goods from one town to another and from one part of the country to another.

These creatures did the job, but they had their drawbacks. Animals could only carry so much so far. They needed to be fed and kept healthy. They needed rest and a place to sleep. And their backbreaking duties often made these animals' lives miserable.

By the 1890s, something new was beginning to appear on country roads and city streets. Makers of the automobile, or horseless carriage, promised it could do the job of one or many animals. At first, some people weren't too sure about these machines. The first automobiles were

Early automobiles weren't always better than horses. This car's narrow wheels are stuck in mud that a horse could easily travel through.

Hold Your Nose and Do the Math

About 175,000 horses lived in New York City in the 1890s. Each horse produced about 30 pounds (14 kilograms) of manure per day. Can you imagine trying to clean up that mess?

No Accidents with The Oldsmobile

Mechanical skill and mathematical exactness eliminate the danger of the horse's uncertain temper, sudden fright and unruly disposition—no "Runaways" with *The Best Thing on Wheels.*

The controlling mechanism is simple, strong and instantly responsive to the will of the driver, giving a sense of perfect security. There is no factor of uncertainty in the Oldsmobile—*"Nothing to watch but the road."*

Price, with Mud Guards, $650.00

Equipped with a motor, running 30 miles on one gallon of gasolene; an improved mixer which guarantees a uniform charge and perfect explosion every time, and strong trussed axles. Call on any of our 58 Selling Agencies or write for illustrated book to Department G.

Olds Motor Works, Detroit, Mich.

loud and smoky. They tended to break down a lot. And they often scared the horses they shared the road with. But as the years passed, automakers learned how to build better, more reliable machines.

Pre-Pickup Days: Aftermarket Conversions

The benefits of the car over the horse were obvious. Cars didn't need food every day. They could carry heavier loads longer distances. They didn't need a comfortable place to sleep. And they didn't leave piles of mess on the roads, either.

In those early years, cars were a bigger focus than trucks. Automakers spent most of their time and energy making passenger cars. Most of the trucks of the early 1900s tended to be big, heavy machines. They were not what most people think of as light-duty trucks. But demand for smaller trucks—often known as delivery wagons—grew.

FINDLEYS WIRELESS CONTROLLED REO SPEEDWAGON
Controlled By Operator In Booth 15 Electrical Building
This Radio Apparatus Installed By Findley Electric Co.

This Speedwagon Can Send or Receive Radio Messages when running at high speed. Learn to tea wireless operator, you will find it interesting a profitable Ask the Radio Man

Demonstration of Wireless Control of Vehicles Course of Reo Speedwagon directed by Radio Operator In Booth 15. Electrical Bldg. Radio Apparatus Installed By Findley Electric Co.

Visit The
ELECTRICAL BLDG.
Radio Exhibit Booth 15

REO
SPEEDWAGON
Fawkes Auto Co.

Reo Motor Car Company started building Speed Wagons in 1915. They had electric starters and electric lights. This Reo Speed Wagon was equipped with a Finley electric radio.

By the first decade of the 1900s, light-duty trucks such as Reo's Speed Wagon and International Harvester Corporation's Model S were finding buyers around the country. Other companies joined in. In 1917 the Ford Motor Company began offering the Model TT truck. Chevrolet introduced its Model 490 truck the following year.

It wouldn't be accurate to call these true pickup trucks, though. Why? Because these machines didn't come

No One Knows

No one knows exactly when the term *pickup* came into popular use. In the early years of the truck business, light-duty pickups were usually called express or express delivery trucks. In 1913 the Studebaker Corporation used the term *pickup* to describe one of its truck lines. No one is sure if this was the first use of the term, however. By the 1930s, *pickup* had become the standard word used to describe these light-duty trucks.

Before automakers made complete factory-built pickups, buyers would have to build the trucks themselves with aftermarket bodies. Ford's 1924 Model TT *(right)* was the first pickup to have a factory-built C cab.

with a cargo bed attached to the back. Instead, automakers built only the chassis. The chassis is the bare bones of the vehicle. It includes the basic mechanical parts such as the engine, wheels, and steering system. These parts are attached to the frame. The beds and bodies were added later by other companies. This process was known as aftermarket conversion. Automakers didn't see much profit in building pickups. But that soon changed as the popularity of these machines grew.

The First True Pickups

By the 1920s, truck chassis were selling by the tens of thousands each year. Aftermarket conversion had become a big business. It was only a matter of time before automakers decided to cash in. In 1924 the Dodge Brothers Motor Vehicle Company of Detroit came out with a light-duty truck that included a cab and bed. A year later, Ford introduced the Model T Runabout with Pick-Up Body. This was a version of Ford's famous Model T with a pickup-style bed and body. Ford's machine was a huge hit. Other automakers, such as General Motor's Chevrolet and GMC divisions soon began making their own factory-built light-duty trucks. The pickup was here to stay.

So what was the difference between, say, the regular Model T car and the Model T pickup? There was more to it than a bed in back. To carry heavy loads, light-duty trucks had stronger frames than the kind found on regular cars. They also had stronger axles and a longer wheelbase (the distance between the car's front and rear axles). But these machines looked like and had many of the same parts as the cars they were based on.

In addition, the first factory-built pickups were all business. Looks and driver comfort were not a priority. The trucks were built for work on the farm, delivering goods, or other jobs. They were a long way from being stylish. Their cabs were cramped and generally uncomfortable.

The Great Depression and World War II

The 1920s were a fabulous time for the auto industry and the United States. The country's economy was doing well, and cars and trucks were selling in huge numbers. But this all came crashing down when the Great Depression (1929–1942) hit in 1929. A complicated series of events led to the collapse of the country's economy.

Even when times were tough during the Great Depression, many Americans still kept their automobiles. This farmer and his truck are returning from a market in Oklahoma.

Mack trucks were known for being big and tough. But their light-duty trucks, such as this 1937 Mack Jr ¾-ton truck, were stylish too.

Businesses and banks closed. Millions of Americans lost their jobs and watched their life savings disappear.

The Great Depression had a huge impact on the auto industry. Few Americans had the money to buy new cars. Many automakers went out of business. The major companies—Ford, Chrysler, and General Motors, known as the Big Three—fought to survive the times.

One way to attract customers was to keep offering new and improved products. By the early 1930s, pickups were no longer just cars with boxes on the back. Automakers were designing

pickups separately from cars and building them as pickups from the ground up. The results were better-looking and better-working trucks. For example, Dodge—which had been purchased by Chrysler—redesigned its pickup for the 1933 model year. The truck had a sloping front grille and big, rounded fenders. It even featured a stylish hood ornament, a leaping ram. It would be a Dodge trademark for many years.

Automakers also developed more powerful engines, such as Ford's flathead V8. More power meant more speed and better hauling and towing ability. Stronger frames, better braking systems, and tougher suspension systems (the parts that attach the wheels to the car) also helped keep customers interested.

By 1941 the Great Depression was coming to an end, but even more troubles were on the horizon. On December 7 of that year, Japanese forces attacked the U.S. Naval Base at Pearl Harbor in the Hawaiian Islands.

How an Internal Combustion Engine Works

Over the years, pickup truck engines have changed in many ways. Most modern pickup trucks have internal combustion V6, V8, or V10 engines. (A V8, *below*, is an engine that includes eight cylinders arranged in the shape of a V.) Like most car engines, they run on gasoline and use a four-stroke cycle (*right*). The four-stroke cycle burns a mixture of air and gas to power the truck. These cycles take place thousands of times per minute inside a truck engine.

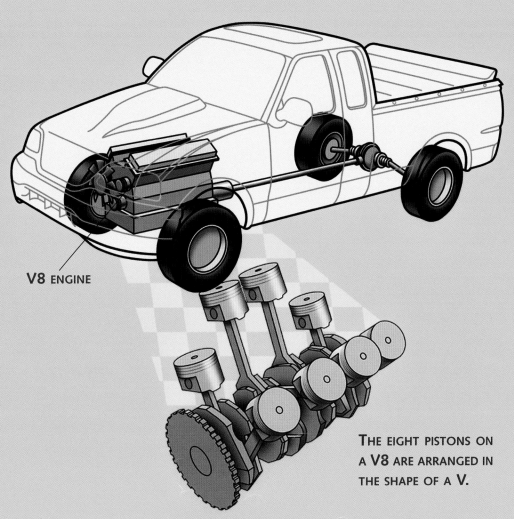

V8 ENGINE

THE EIGHT PISTONS ON A **V8** ARE ARRANGED IN THE SHAPE OF A **V.**

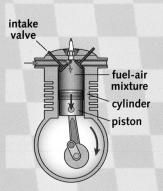

1. INTAKE STROKE
The piston moves down the cylinder and draws the fuel-air mixture into the cylinder through the intake valve.

intake valve
fuel-air mixture
cylinder
piston

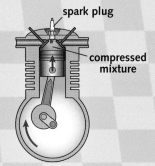

2. COMPRESSION STROKE
The piston moves up and compresses the fuel-air mixture. The spark plug ignites the mixture, creating combustion (burning).

spark plug
compressed mixture

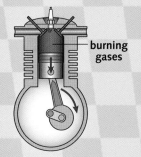

3. POWER STROKE
The burning gases created by combustion push the piston downward. This gives the engine its power.

burning gases

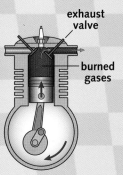

4. EXHAUST STROKE
The piston moves up again and pushes out the burned-out exhaust gases through the exhaust valve.

exhaust valve
burned gases

This is the interior of a 1947 Dodge Power Wagon.

This action drove the United States into World War II (1939–1945). In early 1942, the U.S. government ordered automakers to halt production of new cars. Automotive factories switched over to building equipment—such as trucks, tanks, and aircraft—and materials for the war effort.

Among the most famous truck lines of the war was the Dodge WC-series. This was a line of big, sturdy machines that were built to last. They had four-wheel drive. This meant the engine sent power to all four wheels instead of just the rear wheels. Four-wheel-drive (4x4) trucks had the traction (grip) to slog through tough terrain, such as mud, swamps, rocky hills, and just about anywhere else. The WC-series trucks proved so popular that Dodge sold them for civilian (nonmilitary) use after the war. The company gave its tough and rugged civilian truck the perfect name— Power Wagon.

Coupe Pickups

In the 1920s and 1930s, automakers tried to fill the gap between cars and pickups with cargo box conversions. They were cars that could fit a specially made cargo box in the trunk. The owner of the car could either raise or remove the trunk lid and slide the cargo box in. The box could also be easily removed when it wasn't needed.

Style and Substance: Postwar Pickups

After the war ended, U.S. automakers needed a few years to get back to building all-new civilian vehicles. But trucks that came out in the late 1940s were worth the wait. First in line were the Advance Design series trucks from Chevrolet and GMC. These vehicles had cleaner and more attractive looks than prewar trucks. They featured a more rounded cab and hood, headlights that rested inside of the fenders instead of on top, and a classy front grille. The Advance Design trucks were also more comfortable. They had wider and roomier cabs and more window area for better visibility.

Naturally, Ford, Dodge, and other truck companies weren't far behind. In 1948 Ford offered the first of its attractive F-series trucks, the F-1. Dodge introduced its Pilot House models that same year. The nickname came from the truck's cab. Like the pilothouse on a ship, the truck featured lots of window space for better visibility.

The Big Three weren't the only companies making memorable trucks. In 1949 the Indiana-based Studebaker Corporation unveiled its all-new 2R-series pickup. The cab and bed of this shapely machine flowed together nicely.

An eager public couldn't get enough, and pickup trucks sold by the hundreds of thousands. Competition was fierce between automakers, as each worked hard to outdo the other

with more powerful, roomier, and more stylish trucks. In the 1950s, Chevrolet led the pack as the number one selling pickup truck maker. Ford followed a close second. Dodge cruised along a distant third. Other companies such as International Harvester, Studebaker, Nash, and Willys-Overland fought for the remaining customers.

It is easy to spot the grille of a GMC truck. This is a 1951 model.

Compare the fenders and cargo bed of the 1955 Cameo Carrier *(left)* to those of a regular 1955 Chevy pickup *(right)*.

True Classics: The 1950s

All this competition worked well for customers. Every year, people could look forward to something new and better than before. In 1953 Ford topped everyone else with its brand-new F-100 series pickup. With its tall cab, sloping windshield, and tough-looking front grille, the F-100 became an instant hit. In fact, the machine was so cool that it became a favorite with young people. Many young hot-rodders "souped up" their F-100s, tinkering with the engines to give them extra speed for racing. No doubt about it—pickup trucks weren't just for work anymore.

In 1955 Chevrolet responded to the F-100 with its own line of new trucks. The Task Force pickups featured roomy cabs and eye-catching looks. The truck's mean-looking front end brings to mind a bulldog ready to attack. And if the Task Force trucks weren't cool enough, Chevrolet also offered a special line of stylish trucks called Cameo Carriers. These were Task Force trucks with added touches such as two-tone paint jobs and two-tone interiors. The Cameo trucks also featured a stylish cargo bed with fiberglass sides. The fiberglass was molded to match the fenders of the cab. The result was one of the nicest-looking trucks ever seen at the time. Naturally, Ford and Dodge responded with their own stylish pickups. Ford called its line Styleside trucks, while Dodge named its line the Sweptside.

Chevy's trucks had more than just good looks. The 1955 model year saw the launch of Chevy's famous small-block V8. This high-powered engine left the competition in its dust.

Then in 1957, Ford caught everyone by surprise by introducing a very different sort of pickup—the Ranchero. The Ranchero was more car than truck. In fact, it was a Ford station wagon with a cargo bed instead of a passenger area in back. The Ranchero wasn't a heavy hauler, but it could do light jobs. And it was comfortable and great looking. Two years later, Chevy answered with its El Camino (Spanish for "the road"). It proved to be even more popular than the Ranchero.

A 1964 *(left)* and a 1959 El Camino

The 1960s and 1970s: Smaller Trucks, Faster Trucks

As the 1960s began, Chevrolet was still the best-selling U.S. truck maker. But foreign companies were beginning to attract sales with their own unique models. One of these imported trucks was the Volkswagen Type 2 from Germany. The VWs were compact and got great gas mileage. They were a good match for people who wanted small, thrifty trucks.

The walls on the bed of the VW Type 2 pickup folded down for easier loading and unloading.

The VWs had an unusual design. The cab was set at the very front of the vehicle. Volkswagen put the truck's engine in the rear, underneath the cargo bed. The driver sat directly over the front wheels. (Sitting so far forward helped the driver see the road ahead.) U.S. automakers copied the idea. It became known as forward control. Ford's Econoline and Chevrolet's Corvair 95 appeared in 1961. Dodge followed with its A-100 three years later.

Another 1960s truck trend went in a different direction. Muscle cars—cars with large, powerful engines—were all the rage. Automakers competed with one another to build bigger, more powerful engines. Fast cars were the name of the game. Soon automakers began to offer these engines in trucks too. Horsepower—the unit used to measure an engine's power—became a key selling point. For example, Chevy's C- and K-series pickups could be purchased with huge V8 engines that produced well over 300 horse-power. This was a far cry from the old Model TT truck of the 1910s, which produced just 20 horsepower.

Overall, pickup truck styling changed dramatically from the 1950s to the 1960s. Truck bodies in the 1960s went from being rounded and curvy to flat and squarish. Flat hoods, roofs, and fenders became the new look. This style would go on well into the 1970s.

The muscle craze came to an end in the early 1970s. High horsepower en-gines guzzled lots of gas and made gobs of air pollution. The U.S. govern-ment passed antipollution laws that put the brakes on these powerful engines.

At the same time, world events led to an oil shortage in the United States. Suddenly, Americans were thinking more about gas mileage. Japanese au-tomakers Nissan and Toyota special-ized in building small, fuel-efficient trucks. As these machines became more popular, U.S. automakers joined forces with Japanese companies to

build their own models. The Chevy LUV (Light Utility Vehicle) was built by Isuzu Motors in Japan in the 1970s. Mazda began building Ford's compact Courier during this same period.

The variety of pickup truck choices grew. In 1972 Dodge introduced the first crew cab pickup. This was a full-size truck with a large cab. The cab

Truck bodies in the 1960s became more boxlike.

Pickup trucks with four-wheel drive (4x4), such as this 1984 Chevrolet S-10, became popular for driving off-road, through snow, or on ice.

had two rows of seats instead of one for more passenger space. In later years, even roomier Club Cabs appeared. Pickup trucks had grown to fit just about every lifestyle. They could do the hard work during the week but had room to take the whole family out for fun on the weekend.

Trucks on Top

In the late 1970s, Ford took over the top spot in pickup truck sales. Ford trucks have remained the best-selling vehicles in the United States ever since. Chevrolet pickups hold second place in the truck race, with Dodge a distant third.

In 1987 Dodge created its first mid-size pickup, the Dakota. This machine was a perfect fit for people who needed something bigger than a compact but didn't want a full-size truck. Ford's Ranger and Chevy's Colorado are similar models. In the 1980s, 4x4 pickups also became more popular. Americans liked having the traction and control offered by 4x4 vehicles.

Recent decades have seen many improvements to pickup trucks. Bigger, roomier cabs and more powerful engines are the key selling points. In the 1990s, Dodge introduced the Quad Cab. This was a cab with two rows of seats and four doors instead of two.

All the big Japanese automakers sell their own lines of pickups in the United States. Nissan, Toyota, Honda, and others have given U.S. truck buyers more choices than ever before. The competition has pushed U.S. automakers to keep coming up with new and improved vehicles. One example is Chevrolet's SSR. This vehicle is more car than truck. It's a stylish, sporty pickup with a small cargo bed in back and a big, powerful engine in front. It's a modern take on the classic Ranchero and El Camino.

Meanwhile, automakers keep looking toward the future. The high price of gasoline has many Americans focusing on fuel efficiency. Automakers are rushing to bring hybrid vehicles onto the market. Hybrid engines use both gasoline and electric power to get excellent gas mileage.

Flexible fuel vehicles (FFVs) have engines that can run on both gasoline and a mixture known as E-85. E-85 includes ethanol, a fuel created from corn. Many people think ethanol may be an important fuel for the future. Pickups and other light-duty vehicles are leading the way with this new technology. As the most popular vehicles in the United States, pickups are sure to lead the way for many years to come.

The 2007 Ford Explorer Sport Trac combines features from the Ford Explorer sport-utility vehicle and the F–150 pickup. The Sport Trac includes a cleaner running V6 engine.

Chapter Two

PICKUP TRUCK CULTURE

Pickup trucks have come a long way in the last 100 years. They have grown from simple, clumsy work machines into cutting-edge vehicles with all the latest technology. In the early 1900s, pickup trucks were purchased for work and little else. In recent times, far more people also buy pickups for play.

What's the appeal? It depends on whom you ask. Many people need and love the power that pickups provide.

They are great for towing boats, trailers, campers, and other recreational equipment. Pickups are as important a part of the family vacation as the campground or the cabin.

The pickup's hauling power is a big attraction for weekend warriors. These people spend their weekends doing home improvements, yard work, and many other projects. They need the pickup's cargo space to haul supplies and equipment.

But to say that people buy pickups just for their usefulness wouldn't be correct. Some people don't care if their pickups can haul or tow a thing.

The owner of this classic pickup truck gave it a customized paint job.

They just like the looks of them. Who can argue with that? And many of these same people put a lot of time and energy into turning their stock (straight from the factory) trucks into dream machines.

Customizing and Restoring

Customizing vehicles—adding new parts, unique paint jobs, and many other options—has long been a popular hobby. For pickup truck owners, customizing is a great way to show off their personalities and craftsmanship. Trucks can be customized in countless ways. Options are limited only by a person's imagination—and maybe one's bank account.

Popular pickup truck customizations include one-of-kind paint jobs, chrome trim, and accessories such as fog lights, roll bars, and grille protectors. Some truck owners replace their stock suspensions with big, heavy-duty systems. These changes allow the owner to add oversized tires to give

the truck a big, hulking look. Unique plush interiors and booming stereo systems are also popular options.

Some truck owners prefer to restore their trucks. Restoring a truck means taking an old truck and making it look as if it just came from the factory. Instead of building a one-of-a-kind truck, a restorer tries to make a truck look as good as new. Restoring requires a lot of craftsmanship and attention to detail. It often means scouring junkyards across the country to find rare parts.

The restoring process begins by tracking down a long-lost truck. Often it's a truck that is rusting away in an old barn or garage. After buying the vehicle, the restorer gets down to work. This usually means taking the truck apart down to the bare body and frame. Once this has been done, the restorer cleans and paints every part so it looks brand new. Rust on the body must be sanded off. Holes need to be filled.

This customized truck features an old semi cab on a modern pickup chassis.

Restoring a Classic Pickup Truck

Mike Key rebuilt and customized this 1932 Ford roadster pickup using parts of other Ford vehicles that he had collected over the years. The restoration took two winters. He and his wife, June, have driven the finished pickup all over Great Britain, France, Germany, and Sweden.

1. One of the first jobs for any restoration is to remove the body and the engine from the frame. (The frame is the part of a vehicle that the engine and the body are attached to.) Later, the frame was painted, and the engine, suspension, and wheels were added to form the chassis *(right)*.

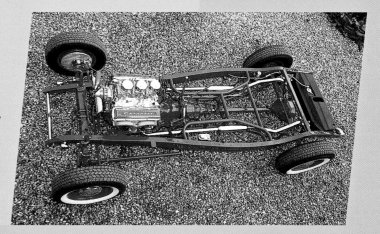

2. Next, work began on the front end. A new frame for the body of the pickup was also built. The front end and the frame were bolted onto the chassis to make sure they fit correctly. They were removed again for painting.

3. The body's exterior was reconstructed on the new frame. Here one of the restorers works on the floor of the body.

4. Here is the completed body and an original Model A pickup bed on the chassis. The restorers later gave the bed a new tailgate and fenders.

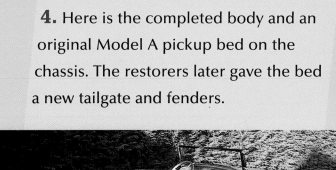

5. The pickup body and bed were prepped and primed—given a coat of special paint that sticks to the metal. The restorer sanded the surfaces before applying another coat of primer. Then the pickup was ready to be painted.

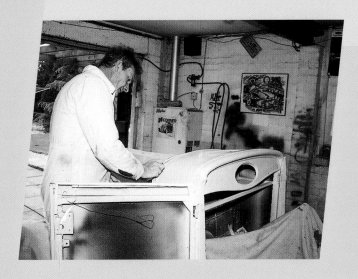

6. The finished product is a gleaming purple roadster pickup with a red interior. Notice how part of the front end was removed to show off the engine.

Classic pickup trucks are lined up at a car show in Saint Paul, Minnesota.

Replacement parts must be tracked down. Once this has been done, the restorer begins the exciting process of putting the truck back together.

Bringing a rusty, old vehicle back to life takes a lot of work. But for some, it's a labor of love. And it's a great feeling to see something old turn into something that looks new again. Once restoring and customizing are done, there is no better place to show off a truck than at a truck show.

Clubs and Shows

Most truck customizers and restorers are members of truck clubs. These groups are located throughout the United States, Canada, and in many other countries. Clubs are a great way for like-minded truck owners to get together and enjoy their favorite machines. Clubs often hold meetings, stage races, and even organize shows where folks can get together to show off their trucks.

Brand Loyalty

Pickup truck owners have always been famous for their brand loyalty. For example, most Ford truck owners are Ford truck owners, plain and simple. They would never even dream of buying a Chevrolet, Dodge, or any other brand of truck. In fact, many brand loyalists look down on folks who own different brands of trucks. These are friendly rivalries, but the feelings often run deep. Pickup truck brand loyalty is usually handed down from generation to generation. For example, many a Chevy truck owner can tell you that his father, grandfather, and even great-grandfather all owned Chevy trucks.

Truck shows are usually held at fairgrounds, in big parking lots, or at other places where a lot of vehicles can be put on display. More often than not, truck shows are part of bigger car shows, where many different kinds of vehicles are showcased.

Shows are a great way for people to get together. Truck owners can check out other trucks and pick up tips and ideas for customizing or restoring. Fans of cars and trucks can wander around checking out all the amazing and beautiful machines. Shows are a great way to bring car and truck lovers together.

Truck Racing

NASCAR® (the National Association of Stock Car Auto Racing) caught on to the truck craze in the mid-1990s. In 1995 NASCAR introduced a racing series that featured modified pickup trucks. The NASCAR Craftsman Truck Series has gone on to become a popular attraction. Truck series races are held on NASCAR tracks such as the Daytona International Speedway and Pocono Raceway. Craftsman Truck Series events are part of a weekend of action. They usually take place on Friday or Saturday before the main NASCAR Nextel Cup race on Sunday.

DID YOU KNOW?
The NASCAR Craftsman Truck Series began as the SuperTruck Series in 1995. It became the Craftsman Truck Series the following year.

Johnny Benson crosses the finish line ahead of Mark Martin during the NASCAR Craftsman Truck Series Conway Freight 200 at the Michigan International Speedway.

The trucks usually race for 150 to 250 miles (241 to 402 km), reaching speeds of up to 190 miles (306 km) per hour.

While the racing machines may look like trucks on the outside, they are actually NASCAR chassis covered with truck-shaped bodies. And the competition between drivers is just as fierce as any kind of stock car racing. Drivers routinely bump, scrape, and "trade paint" with other trucks in traffic—all with an eye toward the winner's circle. The Craftsman Truck Series is a way for truck makers to compete too. Automakers take pride

Craftsman Truck Series Champions

YEAR	DRIVER	MAKE
2006	Todd Bodine	Toyota
2005	Ted Musgrave	Dodge
2004	Bobby Hamilton	Dodge
2003	Travis Kvapil	Chevrolet
2002	Mike Bliss	Chevrolet
2001	Jack Sprague	Chevrolet
2000	Greg Biffle	Ford
1999	Jack Sprague	Chevrolet
1998	Ron Hornaday Jr.	Chevrolet
1997	Jack Sprague	Chevrolet
1996	Ron Hornaday Jr.	Chevrolet
1995	Mike Skinner	Chevrolet

in seeing their trucks win, and having the fastest truck can only help to sell more trucks to the public. The series has become so popular that Japanese automaker Toyota joined the competition in 2004.

NASCAR isn't the only organization that holds truck-racing events. Since the mid-1900s, pickup trucks have been involved in off-road racing. One of the most famous off-road races is the Baja 1000. This 1,000-mile (1,609 km) race runs across the harsh desert of Baja California, the long peninsula (piece of land that projects out into a body of water) off the western coast of Mexico. Pickup trucks, motorcycles, cars, and other vehicles typically race a loop from Ensenada, Mexico, in the north, down the peninsula and back up again. The races are exciting but challenging. Drivers must push their vehicles to the limit in brutal desert heat, on some of the roughest terrain in North America.

A crowd watches driver Gustavo Vildosola fly through the air in his pickup truck during a Trophy Truck race at the SCORE Baja 1000.

The monster truck known as Snake Bite crushes cars at a monster truck rally. Fans can identify their favorite monster trucks by their customized paint jobs.

Monster Trucks

Over the years, pickup trucks have always been linked to power and toughness. And few trucks are tougher or more powerful than monster trucks. Monster truck competitions are a unique sport. They feature trucks that have been transformed into massive machines with giant tires. Monster truck events include races, car crushing, and freestyle competitions. During freestyle competitions, the high-powered machines do tricks such as wheelies, spins, and jumps.

Monster truck bodies may look like stock pickups, but they are one-of-a-kind creations. The bodies are made of a very light but strong material called carbon fiber. They are molded into their unique shape. Underneath the body, monster trucks have custom-made chassis that are built to take the punishment of both races and freestyle competitions. With tires as tall as 66 inches (168 centimeters) and powerful engines that produce as much as 1,500 horsepower, monster trucks certainly deserve their name.

Hays Antique Truck Museum

The history of trucks in the United States is fascinating. And the best place to learn about it is at the Hays Antique Truck Museum in Woodland, California. The museum has the largest collection of antique trucks in the country. It features more than 100 trucks of all kinds, including many historic pickup trucks.

A. W. Hays, a retired trucking company owner, founded the museum in 1982. Hays wanted to preserve the great history of American trucks. A talented craftsman, Hays restored many of the trucks in the collection before he died in 1992. The museum's exhibits feature trucks from nearly every U.S. truck maker, from Chevrolet and International Harvester to Ford and Reo. A visit to the

museum is like taking a step back in time. The museum can remind anyone of how far the pickup truck has come in the last 100 years.

A 1922 Macdonald truck from the Hays Antique Truck Museum in Woodland, California

Hays Antique Truck Museum

To see pictures of some of the trucks in the Hays collection, visit the museum's website at http://www.truckmuseum.org

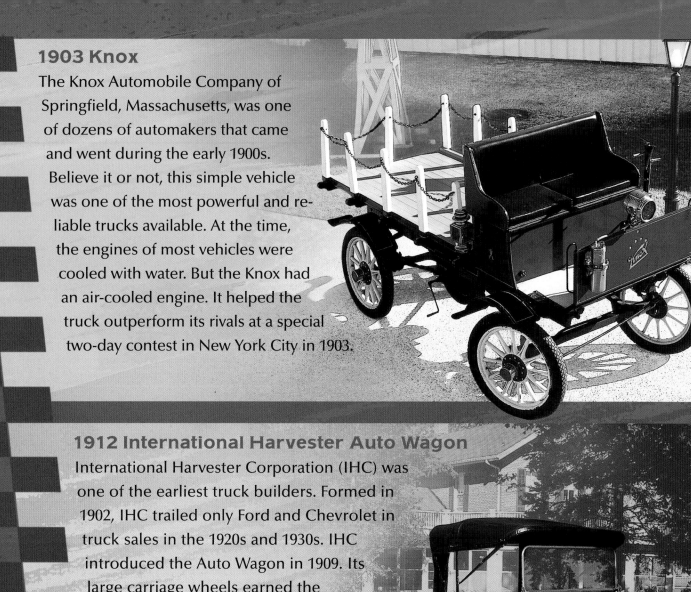

1903 Knox

The Knox Automobile Company of Springfield, Massachusetts, was one of dozens of automakers that came and went during the early 1900s. Believe it or not, this simple vehicle was one of the most powerful and reliable trucks available. At the time, the engines of most vehicles were cooled with water. But the Knox had an air-cooled engine. It helped the truck outperform its rivals at a special two-day contest in New York City in 1903.

1912 International Harvester Auto Wagon

International Harvester Corporation (IHC) was one of the earliest truck builders. Formed in 1902, IHC trailed only Ford and Chevrolet in truck sales in the 1920s and 1930s. IHC introduced the Auto Wagon in 1909. Its large carriage wheels earned the truck the nickname high-wheeler. Its two rear seats could be removed to create cargo space. The leather canopy that protected the front seat from sun and rain was also removable.

1918 Chevrolet Model 490 Light Delivery

Based on the popular Chevrolet 490 car, the 490 was usually built and sold without bodywork. The cab and bed came as an aftermarket conversion. Wooden bodywork, as shown here, was an option for some. This truck was equipped with a four-cylinder engine that produced 26 horsepower. Many modern pickup truck engines have eight-cylinder engines that produce more than 300 horsepower.

1927 Ford Model T Runabout

Introduced in 1908, Henry Ford's Model T car changed the world. Its high quality and low price gave millions of people their first chance to own a car. For years, people who needed trucks adapted their Model Ts with aftermarket conversions. Finally, in 1925, Ford decided to get in on the action. The company offered its first complete pickup truck—the Model T Runabout.

1937 Studebaker Coupe Express

The Studebaker Corporation's history dates back to long before the automobile was invented. The South Bend, Indiana, company switched from building horse-drawn carriages to automobiles in the early 1900s. The model shown here is the Coupe Express. It is basically the company's Dictator passenger car with a cargo box. Although attractive, the truck did not sell well. Studebaker built the Coupe Express for only three years, from 1937 to 1939.

1940 Studebaker Champion Coupe Delivery

Placing a removable cargo box in a coupe style car's trunk was an easy way to make a light-duty truck. Chevrolet, Ford, Plymouth, and other companies experimented with the "coupe delivery" idea in the 1920s and 1930s. Not many were sold, however, and these cars became rare collector's items. The car pictured here is a coupe delivery version of Studebaker's popular Champion model car.

1947 Dodge Power Wagon

This tough and dependable Dodge truck earned its fame during World War II. The huge, powerful 4x4 could go just about anywhere under any conditions. The civilian version was more or less the same as the military model. The beast may not have been pretty, but it pulled and hauled like no other pickup available. Dodge produced the Power Wagon with few changes from 1946 to 1968.

1948 Ford F-1

Ford's F-1 was part of the company's F-series of pickups introduced in 1948. The F-1 was the smallest of the group. Larger models bore the name F-2, F-3, and so on. Ford called its line of trucks Bonus Built. This implied that buyers were getting more for their money compared to other trucks. The truck's attractive styling and roomy cab made it an instant hit. Its classic looks have also made the Ford F-1 a very popular model for collectors.

1954 Chevrolet 3100

After World War II, Chevrolet was the first of the Big Three to come out with an all-new pickup. The Advance Design models were introduced in the summer of 1947 to widespread praise. Chevy's new truck had a roomier cab, larger windows, and wider door openings. The 3100 shown here is a 1954 model—the last full year of the Advance Design trucks. Changes to the 1954 models included updated grilles and curved windshields.

1956 Ford F-100

In the early 1950s, Ford was a distant second to Chevrolet in pickup sales. So the company went all out to regain the lead. Ford spent a whopping $30 million to completely rethink and redesign its pickup truck line. The result arrived in 1953 as the F-100. It is one of the all-time classic trucks and one of the best-looking pickups ever built. The truck shown here is a 1956 model.

1957 Chevrolet 3100 Cameo Carrier

Ford's F-100 was a hit, but it failed to knock Chevrolet off the top spot for truck sales. That's because Chevy came out with its own showstopping line of new trucks in 1955. The Task Force trucks were just as cool as the F-100. The truck shown here is a Cameo Carrier model. Cameo Carriers featured elegant carlike styling. On this 1957 model, note the chrome trim, two-color paint job, hood ornaments, and the smooth fenders on the cargo box.

1957 Dodge D100 Sweptside

Dodge struggled to keep up with the competition in the 1950s. By the middle of the decade, the company ranked fifth in truck sales behind Chevy, Ford, IHC, and GMC. With looks becoming a selling point for truck buyers, Dodge tried its hand at making its own stylish machine. The 1957 D100 Sweptside's smooth cargo box fenders were taken from a Dodge station wagon. A two-tone paint job, chrome trim, and wraparound rear window completed the look.

1957 Ford Ranchero

In the 1950s, pickups began to offer more and more carlike features. So it was only natural that automakers would try working in the other direction—making a car a truck. Enter the Ford Ranchero in 1957. The truck—or was it a car?—was basically a Ford station wagon with part of the roof chopped off. The Ranchero had a cargo bed in place of the rear passenger seats. The vehicle's two-tone paint job and sleek looks made it a popular choice for light jobs around town.

1959 Volkswagen Type 2

The clever design of Volkswagen's Type 2 truck put the cab at the very front of the truck. This gave the driver better visibility and left more room for the cargo bed. The key to the design was the placement of the engine. It was set in the middle of the truck with the cargo bed on top. Drop-down panels on the sides and rear made for easy loading. The Type 2 truck never quite caught on with the U.S. public, however, and sales were poor.

1961 Chevrolet Corvair 95 Rampside

The unusual design of the Volkswagen Type 2 caught the attention of U.S. automakers. By 1961 both Chevrolet and Ford were building trucks using the forward control idea. The Corvair 95 shared the Volkswagen's mid-engine design. The Rampside's unique drop-down side ramp made for easy loading and unloading. The 95 stood for the truck's short 95-inch (241 cm) wheelbase.

1963 Ford Econoline

Like the Corvair 95, the Ford Econoline pickup was a response to the Volkswagen pickup. But Ford chose to place the engine in the front of the truck instead of in the rear. This left more room for a bigger, deeper cargo bed. The affordable Econoline proved the most popular of the forward control trucks. The 1963 model shown here was the best selling of the bunch. Ford stopped building this model in 1967.

1965 Dodge A-100 Little Red Wagon

Dodge was the last of the Big Three to build a forward control truck. The A-100 was launched in 1964. The one shown here has been heavily modified for drag racing. Driver Bill "Maverick" Golden replaced his truck's small six-cylinder engine with a powerful V8. He set the engine behind the cab, added fat racing tires, a roll cage, and much more. The truck was so powerful that it could pop crowd-thrilling wheelies.

1970 Chevrolet El Camino SS 454

El Caminos of this period were based on the popular Chevelle car model. In 1970 the muscle car craze was at its peak. So it was only natural that Chevrolet would stuff its most powerful engine into its El Camino. The result was the SS (Super Sport) 454. The 450-horsepower, 454-cubic-inch (7,440 cubic cm) engine was one of the largest and most powerful of the day.

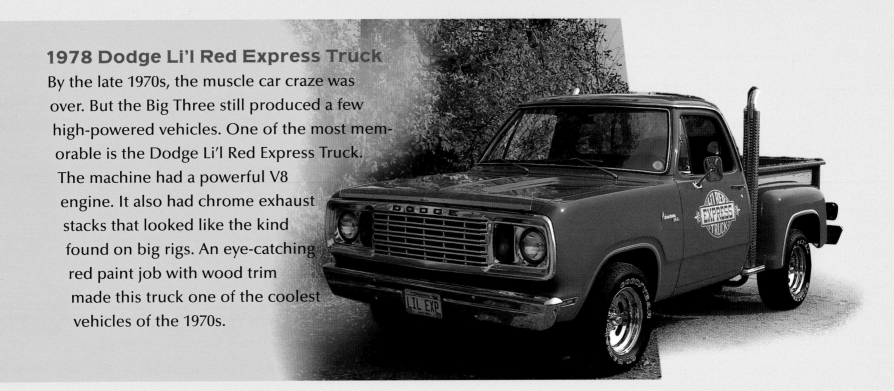

1978 Dodge Li'l Red Express Truck

By the late 1970s, the muscle car craze was over. But the Big Three still produced a few high-powered vehicles. One of the most memorable is the Dodge Li'l Red Express Truck. The machine had a powerful V8 engine. It also had chrome exhaust stacks that looked like the kind found on big rigs. An eye-catching red paint job with wood trim made this truck one of the coolest vehicles of the 1970s.

1996 Dodge Ram Sport

For decades, Dodge had lagged far behind Ford and Chevy in truck sales. Yet the company continued to try new things to get the attention of truck owners. In late 1993, Dodge unleashed the Ram, a redesigned pickup with a tough new look. The Ram's wide face brings to mind huge semitrucks. While not everyone liked the look, the Ram proved to be a big hit, giving Dodge a big boost in truck sales.

2001 Ford SVT Lightning

What do you do when your pickup is the best-selling vehicle in the United States for more than 20 years? How about trying something adventurous? The Ford Special Vehicle Team (SVT) came up with the 380-horsepower 2001 SVT Lightning. It is a juiced-up F-150. The truck's big V8 engine gets extra power from a supercharger. This device creates more horsepower by forcing more air into the engine's cylinder. A killer paint job makes this truck a real stunner.

2004 Chevrolet SSR

Is this machine *really* a pickup truck? Probably not. It does have a small cargo bed in back, though. And the truck's chassis is based on a Chevy Trailblazer sport-utility vehicle. But the SSR's trucklike qualities end there. With a retractable roof, cushy carlike interior, and a massive 400-horsepower V8 engine, this machine was made to tear up the streets. And it looks mighty good doing it too.

2006 Dodge Ram Daytona

Automakers like to offer special edition packages to generate a buzz. The Dodge Ram Daytona is based on the 1969 Dodge Daytona, one of the most famous muscle cars of all time. Like the old Daytona car, the Ram truck has a racy look. The rear spoiler wing on the back of the truck is similar to the car's rear spoiler. The wing works like an upside-down airplane wing. Air flows over it, creating downforce. The downforce keeps the rear end stable at high speeds.

2006 NASCAR Craftsman Truck Series Toyota Tundra

Toyota entered the popular NASCAR Craftsman Truck Series (CTS) in 2004. The Tundra had instant success, winning four races that season. Toyota trucks went on to win nine races the following year and twelve in 2006. The Tundra CTS truck has a V8 engine that produces 675 horsepower. Mike Skinner is driving the Tundra at right.

Glossary

aftermarket conversion: to change or add to a previously manufactured product

bed: the open cargo area, or box, that is the rear of a pickup truck

cab: the closed part in the front of a pickup truck where the driver and passengers sit

chassis: the basic parts of a vehicle, usually the frame and suspension

frame: the structure on which a vehicle is built. The suspension, engine, drive train, and body of a car or truck are all attached to the frame

model year: the particular year that a vehicle is produced. For U.S. automakers, the model year begins a few months before the calendar year. For example, cars for the 1968 model year became widely available in late 1967.

sport-utility vehicle: a 4x4 vehicle that is designed for both on-road and off-road use. It is also called an SUV.

stock: factory produced without modifications

suspension: the parts that connect the wheels to the chassis to the car

wheelbase: the distance between a vehicle's front and rear axles

Selected Bibliography

Brownell, Tom. *Ford Pickup Color History*. Osceola, WI: Motorbooks International, 1994.

Coffey, Frank, and Joseph Layden. *America on Wheels: The First 100 Years: 1896–1996*. Los Angeles: General Publishing Group, 1996.

Mueller, Mike. *Chevrolet Pickups*. Saint Paul: Motorbooks International, 2004.

———. *Pickup Trucks*. Saint Paul: Motorbooks International, 2003.

Rasmussen, Henry. *The Great American Pickup*. Osceola, WI: Motorbooks International, 1997.

Statham, Steve. *Dodge Pickup Trucks*. Osceola, WI: Motorbooks International, 1998.

———. *Henry Ford*. Minneapolis: Lerner Publications Company, 2007.

Further Reading

Buckley, James. *NASCAR*. New York: Dorling Kindersley, 2005.

Johnstone, Michael. *Monster Trucks*. Minneapolis: Lerner Publications Company, 2002.

Zuehlke, Jeffrey. *Classic Cars*. Minneapolis: Lerner Publications Company, 2007.

Websites

Automobiles by Chevrolet
http://www.chevrolet.com/
Check out the newest Chevy trucks, including the Silverado, Colorado, Avalanche, and SSR.

Dodge
http://www.dodge.com/
Dodge's official website has information on the company's newest models of trucks, including the popular full-size Ram pickups and the midsize Dakota.

Ford Vehicles: Truck Showroom
http://www.fordvehicles.com/trucks/
Learn more about the latest models of Ford trucks, including the best-selling F-150 and the midsize Ranger.

NASCAR.COM: Craftsman Truck Series
http://www.nascar.com/series/truck/
Get the latest news and results for the NASCAR Craftsman Truck Series from the official NASCAR website.

Index

aftermarket conversions, 10, 35

automobiles, history of, 7–8, 11–12, 14, 18, 19, 21, 36

Baja 1000, 31

beds, 4, 10, 11, 14, 15, 16, 17, 18, 21, 27, 35, 36, 39, 40, 41, 44

Big Three automakers, 12, 15, 38, 42, 43

bodies, 10, 11, 19, 24, 26–27, 30, 32, 35

cabs, 4, 10, 11, 14, 15, 16, 19–20, 35, 37, 38, 40, 42; Club Cabs, 20; crew cabs, 19–20; Quad Cabs, 20

cargo boxes. See beds

chassis, 10, 26, 27, 30, 32, 44

Chevrolet (Chevy), 11, 14, 15, 16, 17, 18, 19, 20, 29, 30, 33, 34, 36, 38, 39, 41, 43; Advance Design series, 14–15; Cameo Carriers, 16–17, 39; Colorado, 20; Corvair 95 Rampside, 18, 41; C-series, 18; El Camino, 17, 21; El Camino SS 454, 42; K-series, 18; LUV, 19; Model 490 light delivery, 9, 35; Silverado, 5; small-block V8 engine, 17; SSR, 21, 44; S-10, 20; Task Force, 16, 39

Chrysler, 12

coupe pickups, 14, 36

delivery wagons, 8–9

Dodge, 10, 12, 14, 15, 17, 18, 19, 20, 29, 30, 37, 39, 42, 43; A-100, 18, 42; crew cab, 19–20; Dakota, 20; D100 Sweptside, 39; Li'l Red Express, 43; Pilot House, 15; Power Wagon, 14, 37; Ram, 5, 43; Ram Daytona, 45; Sweptside, 17; WC-series, 14

engines, 10, 12, 13, 18–19, 20, 21, 27, 33, 34, 35, 40, 41, 42, 43, 44, 45; air-cooled, 34; Chevy small-block V8, 17; Ford flathead V8, 12; hybrid, 21; internal combustion, 13; LS6 454, 42

fenders, 12, 14, 16, 17, 19, 27, 39

flexible fuel vehicles (FFVs), 21

Ford, 9, 10–11, 12, 15, 16, 17, 20, 29, 30, 33, 34, 35, 36, 37, 38, 39, 41, 43; Courier, 19; Econoline, 18, 41; Explorer Sport Trac, 21; flathead V8 engine, 13; F-1, 15, 37; F-100 series, 16, 38, 39; F-150, 4, 5, 21, 44; F-series, 5, 15, 37; Model A, 27; Model T car, 10, 11, 35; Model T Runabout, 10–11, 35; Model TT, 9, 19; 1932 Roadster pickup, 26–27; Ranchero, 17, 21, 40; Ranger, 20; Styleside, 17; SVT Lightning, 44

forward control, 18, 40–42

four-wheel drive (4x4), 14, 20, 37

frames, 10, 11, 12, 24, 26, 27

General Motors Company (GMC), 11, 12, 14, 15, 39

Golden, Bill "Maverick," 42

Great Depression, 11–12

grilles, 12, 15, 16, 38

Hays, A. W., 33

Hays Antique Truck Museum, 33

heavy-duty trucks, 8, 33

Honda, 20

hoods, 12, 14, 19, 39

horsepower, 18–19, 33, 35, 42, 44, 45

horses, 6–7, 8

hot-rodders, 16

hybrid vehicles, 21

International Harvester Corporation (IHC), 9, 15, 33, 34; Auto Wagon, 34; Model S, 9

Isuzu, 19

Japanese automakers, 19, 20, 31

Knox Automobile Company, 34

lights, 9, 14, 24

Mack, 12

Mazda, 19

monster trucks, 32–33

muscle cars, 18, 19, 42, 43

NASCAR Craftsman Truck Series, 29–31, 45

Nash, 15

Nissan, 19, 20

off-roading, 20, 31

pickup trucks: brand loyalty, 29; carlike design, 10, 11, 14, 17, 21, 36, 39, 40, 44; clubs, 28; compact, 19; definition of, 4; gas mileage of, 18, 19, 21; history of, 4, 8–21, 33, 34–45; mid-size, 20; names, 8, 9; restoring and customizing, 23, 24–28, 29; shows, 28–29; uses for, 4, 11, 22–23

racing, 16, 29–31, 32, 42, 45

Reo Motor Car Company, 9, 33; Speed Wagon, 9

Skinner, Mike, 45

sport-utility vehicles (SUVs), 21, 44

Studebaker, 9, 15, 36; Champion Coupe Delivery, 36; Coupe Express, 36; 2R-series, 15

suspensions, 12, 24, 26

Toyota, 19, 20, 30, 31, 45; Tundra, 45

two-tone paint, 16, 39, 40

Volkswagen, 18; Type 2, 18, 40, 41

wheelbase, 11, 41

Willys-Overland, 15

World War II, 12, 14, 38

About the Author

Jeffrey Zuehlke is a writer and editor. He has written more than a dozen nonfiction books for children. He lives in Minneapolis.

About the Consutant

Mike Mueller is an automotive writer and photographer. He has written and photographed more than thirty books on automotive history. He lives in Atlanta.

Photo Acknowledgments

The images in this book are used with the permission of: Ford Motor Company, p. 5; © Getty Images, pp. 6 (background), 11, 30, 45 (bottom); Library of Congress, p. 6 (LC-USZ62-96212); © ATD Group, Inc./Artemis Images, p. 7; Copyright 2006 GM Corp. Used with permission, GM Media Archive, pp. 8, 20; Charles J. Hibbard, Minnesota Historical Society, p. 9; www.ronkimballstock.com, pp. 10, 21, 40 (bottom), 44 (bottom); © Mike Mueller, pp. 12, 14, 16, 17, 33, 34 (both), 35 (both), 36 (both), 37 (both), 38 (both), 39 (both), 40 (top), 41 (top), 42 (both), 43 (both), 44 (top), 45 (top); © Laura Westlund/Independent Picture Service, p. 13; © Mike Key, pp. 15, 18, 23, 26 (all), 27 (all), 41 (bottom); © Jerry Heasley, p. 19; © PhotoEquity/Artemis Images, p. 22 (background); © Lester Lefkowitz/CORBIS, p. 24; © Lauren Wilken/Independent Picture Service, pp. 25, 28; © Vildosola Racing/Artemis Images, p. 31; © Duomo/CORBIS, p. 32.

Front Cover: www.ronkimballstock.com.